HOW TO DEAL RUTHLESSLY WITH HOUSE HOLD ENEMIES

BY

BISHOP OCHEI INNOCENT

Co

DEDICATION

This book is dedicated to those who study what they read or hear.

"Watch and pray that you fall not into temptation."

Mathew 26:41

WHY ARE HOUSEHOLD ENEMIES DANGEROUS?

1. They know you inside out including all your secrets and weak points.
2. You are bonded together by strong ties of blood, water, language and land.

3. You eat and drink together.
4. They hear you pray and take note
    of your heart desires.
5. Sometimes they are the first, if not
    only ones you share your dreams,
    visions, plans and projects with.
6. They know your financial status.
7. They might also know you
    spiritual strength or none of it.
8. They know your associates and
    perhaps friends.
9. Therefore, when they choose to
    move against you, they know what
    to do or where to go or how best to
    fight the war before you know
    what hit you.
10.   You are used to their smiles,
    so you rarely notice the small
    frowns they give, so the element of
    total surprise is on their side.
11. They go to war behind your back
    and/or when you least expect.

12. Suddenly, nothing around you
    seems to work and affliction
    begins to arise not just twice but
    serially.

    What can one do under the
    circumstances?

    The Bible tells me that there is
    nothing new under the sun and
    that there is nothing comes to us
    that have not befallen another
    person before.
     So, why not we go deeper into this
    and unmask the solution?

"AND A HOUSEHOLD"PERSON'S ENEMIES WILL THOSE OF HIS OWN HOUSE HOLD.

MATHEW 10:36

CHAPTER ONE

CAN YOU BELIEVE THIS?

John's wife had problems conceiving. He took her to see so many doctors all to no avail. Doctors themselves were perplexed because all medical tests showed that the wife had not known problem.

She just could not conceive.

They say a problem shared is a problem solved. In the process of running here and there, the couple met somebody who recommended a Deliverance Minister and they went to see him.

In the course of the ministration, the prophet told them that the person responsible for their pains is no one else than the wife's mother.

Incidentally, she was with them at the counseling session. She had been the "chief sympathizer" for the couple over their predicament. Sometimes, she "wept" louder than the bereaved.

Little did the couple know that all the mother-in-law's tears were noting but crocodile tears. On the mother-in-law's part, there was no where she did not take the young couple. In fact, she had been the one searching out almost all the churches and places that look like church they had gone to over time.

There was no room for argument. The Bible says that prayer is the key to all things. The Prophet being an experienced man, did not bother to ask the elderly woman what her opinion was about his finding. Rather he went into more prayers in the course of which, the mother-in-law confessed her witchcraft and consultations to native doctors that tied up the womb of the daughter.

The Bibles says that a man's worst enemies are often members of his own house-hold.

The troubles with that are:

1. **We love members of our household so much** that we can hardly doubt their own love for us. Due to the fact that we genuinely love them, we give trust to them. We cannot for the same reason think harm towards them and because we are not capable of doing that, we believe that all minds are the same.

But the Book of Jeremiah tells me that the heart of man is desperately wicked: who can know it.

2. **We probably grew up with them and they fought battles with us against outsiders.** In all things, even when we were wrong, they sided with us. So we believe than when the chips are down, things will continue to be as they were and those so close to us can never change but it has been empirically proven that people do change as they grow up and come under other influences. Handy example are couples that end up in divorce courts. At the outset, they were so much in love that even they themselves could never ever believe that any thing would go

wrong but it did and they ended up with divorce certificates.

3. **Blood is thicker than water.** Most members of our household are our blood relations, often siblings and we believe that we are so bonded by blood as to merit trust forever. Sooner than later, we realize that we were only building castles in the air.

Who would ever think that a mother would be against her own daughter to the extent of tying up the womb of the young one?

Many of us find ourselves in difficulties that we can neither label nor decode. We pray but these things keep recurring. It is as if someone is listening to our prayer points and actually countering them. Sometimes, you discover belatedly that once you discuss a business project of expected profit or blessing with particular relatives, the thing must surely fail.

Have these things not happened to you? What did you do to solve such challenge? Perhaps you know someone it happened to and still does? What really should a man do to come out of such ugly situation?

"WHEN THE LORD TAKES PLEASURE IN ANYONE'S WAY, HE CAUSES THEIR ENEMIES TO MAKE PEACE WITH THEM."

PROVERBS 16:7

CHAPTER TWO

REASONS WHY MEMBERS OF A PERSON'S HOUSEHOLD CAN BE AGAINST HIM OR HER.

1. **This often happens when you marry outside their consent.**
   To date and in many lands and

climes, some still believe that an intending couple has no right to choose bride or groom for themselves. Some believe that marriage is a family to family affair with little or no say from the people who will eventually have to live with one another. When eventually, there comes a young boy or girl who goes out of the norm to pick a bride or groom on his or her own, there could be a member who feels so aggrieved that he or she takes the law into his or her own hands.

2. **Envy is another known factor.** This happens more in polygamous homes. Envy comes in when one mother feels that the child of the other woman is progressing more than hers. Before you know it, she starts running from pillar to post

in search of something harmful to do to the progressing one.

We have also had situations in which two fathers feel bothered about the supremacy of the other person's child and to ensure there is a change, resort to black magic.

3. **Sibling's rivalry can be another factor.** This is when envy takes control among children born of same parents. This is often the result of poor upbringing. You see children of the same parents competing to the extent that harm one another.

Recently, I got hold of a Nigerian newspaper. It told the story of two brothers of same parents: born into a monogamous home. The younger brother was arrested by the police for murdering the elder brother.

When asked why he killed his brother, the murder accused their father of favoring the dead one in all things. For instance, he said the father sent the other one to school but sent him to the farm! Rightly or wrongly, sinners always have a reason for their sin.

4. **Another factor is blackmail.** This happens when a member of the household goes into a cult group or witchcraft. In this case, leaders of the cult or coven might ask the member of the household to harm one of his relatives in order to climb in rank or to prove his or her loyalty!

Still talking about newspapers I also read of a young man who killed his elder brother for the reason that the cult he belonged to asked him to do so in order to prove his loyalty.

5. **Greed is a major player** in the challenge or problem of household enemies. When people desire what they refuse to acquire by hard work, they can do anything to get what they want especially when money and sex are involved. This is why it often takes an insider to conspire with outsiders for the kidnap of a person. It takes a person who knows that there gold and diamond accessories in a safe, for robbers to come in a steal it. As they say in Africa, it is the rat at home that normally tells the rat outside that there is fish in the rafter. When a person is greedy, he will be driven by that greed to the extent that he or she loses his or her bubbles.

6. **Demonic possession is another factor**. When people are possessed, they do what the demon says and not reason at all. This includes satanic control of a person. Have you ever visited the condemned criminals' wing of any prison or correction center? The common excuse is "the devil deceived me" or ***"Satan made me do it"***. Others simply say: "I do not know what came over me". The Bible tells me that the devil is roaming about looking for whom to devour.

7. **Wickedness can be a major problem**. The Bible says that the heart of man is desperately wicked who can know it. Some are born with a heart of stone. They simply are incapable of loving anyone. Not even their family members.

They have neither self control nor conscience. They do whatever it takes to achieve their goals including hurting or depriving their loved ones or those that love them.

"FOR HE THAT SPEAKS IN AN
TONGUE SPEAKS NOT UNTO
MEN, BUT UNTO GOD: FOR NO
MAN UNDERSTANDS, HOW BE IT
IN THE SPIRIT HE SPEAKS
MYSTERIES.'

1 CORINTHIANS 14:2

CHAPTER THREE
THE WAY OUT

To be free of household enemies, we just have to do the following"

1. **Fight ignorance**.
   Hosea 4: says "My people perish for lack of knowledge. When we do not even know what is going one, how can we fight it? That is why a Christian must not play with Bible study. He or she must get acquainted to the scriptures both to know his rights as a child of God and the limits of the adversary Satan's power. He or she must also be conversant with the devices of the devil. He or she

should be aware that devil is the one that makes people, including our loved ones to give us offense.

2. **Watch, do not sleep.** The bible says; watch and pray that you fall not into temptation. The sole duty of Satan is to roam to and fro the earth looking for the unwary that he will devour. We must therefore as Christians, be vigilant. Watch your siblings closely. Are they all in the Lord? Who are their friends? They say tell me with whom you go and I will tell you what you are. Who is greedy or without self control? Etc.

Do not be careless. This will enable you get some early

warnings. Do they not say a stitch in time saves nine?

3. **Run to the Lord.**
The Bible tells me that the name of the Lord is a strong tower and those who run under it are protected. Some trust in horses and chariots but a wise man seeks the Lord because there is no help in any other name than Jesus Christ which is the only name given unto man that who so ever believes in him shall be saved.

When a person begins to notice strange happenings and suspects that his activities and prayers are being monitored and attacked, his first port of call should be nowhere else than before the Lord God of Hosts.

The Psalmist says I look up to the Hill from whence comes my help. The Lord himself says look unto me all you who labor and I will give you rest. A third scripture, and which I quoted earlier, says that the name of the Lord is a strong tower and those who run under it they are protected.

4. **Pray without season or ceasing.** Cry unto the Lord. Present your case to Him. Pour out your heart. Mathew 7:7 says: **ask and you shall be given.** Ask the Lord to intervene in your affairs and he surely will. There is nothing prayers cannot do. Psalm 81:10

says: ***"Open your mouth wide and I will fill it.***" Take authority in the name of Jesus Christ to bind and loose your destiny from the bondage of those fighting you. The Bible says that there is no enchantment against Jacob and you are surely a seed of Jacob. Therefore, no weapon formed or fashioned against you shall prosper. Open your mouth and declare it for confession brings possession.

5. **Be slow to speak.** Mind who you share your visions and dreams with. We are told in the Bible book of James that we should be slow to speak. Be more a man of prayer and action. Speak less. Remember that the problem of Joseph the

son of Jacob started from the day he shared his dreams with his brothers. What was the result? They conspired and sold him into slavery! Learn from the mistakes of others and become reserved.

6. **Separate yourself.** There is a reason why God separated Abraham from his father's house. If you notice that you and your siblings or household are not on the same page regarding issues of life or spiritual matters, separate yourself because light and darkness have nothing in common. Go where you are celebrated and not where you are tolerated.

7. **Speak in tongues when you pray.** This will help you confuse monitoring spirits and listening human ears. The Bible tells me that when we pray in tongue, Satan is confused. If Satan can be so confused, what do you think will happen to his agents under such condition? They will be in chaos and anarchy! Speak in tongue as often as the Holy Spirit leads you. The Bible tells me that when we speak in tongue, the Holy Spirit intercedes for us. So why not take advantage of that?

LET US PRAY?

Father God I thank you for opening my eyes to the dangers of household enemies.

Open my eyes to see in time that which can be prevented.

Help me to pray without ceasing and never allow me to be ashamed.

Separate me from the wicked and may all their evil plans fall upon their head unless they repent of their sins.

Do not allow my enemies to say where is my God? Arise in my affairs, I pray in the name of Jesus Christ and grant me victory over the wicked no matter who they are. Amen.

NOTES

NOTES

NOTES

NOTES

THANKS FOR READING THROUGH.

SHOULD YOU HAVE A NEED FOR PRAYERS, PLEASE EMAIL ME AT;
newochei@gmail.com
I ALSO ENCOURAGE YOU TO REACH ME WITH SUGGESTIONS YOU HAVE FOR THE IMPROVEMENT OF THIS BOOK IN THE NEXT EDITION.YOU CAN ALSO LEAVE AN HONEST REVIEW ON AMAZON.

ONCE MORE I THANK YOU FOR CHOOSING TO READ THIS BOOK AND I PRAY THAT ONE WORD

REMAINS IN YOU LIFE FROM THIS
LITTLE BOOK.

=BISHOP OCHEI INNOCENT.

OTHER BOOKS BY THE SAME AUTHOR

1. HOW TO DEAL RUTHLESSLY WITH THE SPIRIT OF CONSPIRACY.
2. HOW TO DEAL RUTHLESSLY WITH SIN.
3. HOW TO DEAL RUTHLESSLY WITH USE AND DUMP SPIRIT.

15. WHY MANY PROPHETS HAVE SMALL CONGREGATIONS.